STAIN MY DAYS BLUE

(a collection of poems)

PATRICIA A. JOHNSON

AUSDOH PRESS

Philadelphia, PA   1999

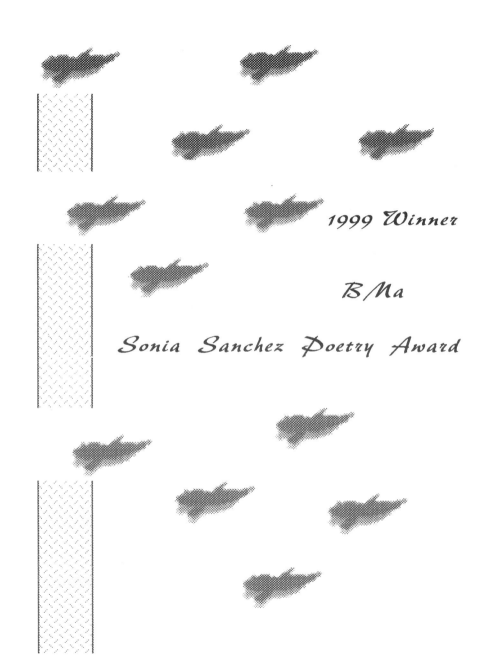

1999 Winner

B/Ma

Sonia Sanchez Poetry Award

For information about permission to reproduce selections from this book, write to Permissions, **Ausdoh Press**, Post Office Box 42863, Philadelphia, Pennsylvania, 19101.

Grateful acknowledgement to the magazines and journals in which the following poems first appeared:

BMA: THE SONIA SANCHEZ LITERARY REVIEW: Sister Moon, Somebody's Child, Gabriel, Witness, Crystal, Conjurer Woman, Spoon, Word Bone
CELEBRATION (an anthology): Spirit Rising
LONZIE'S FRIED CHICKEN: Sisters, Calling for Snow, Breath on my Fingers
OBSIDIAN II: BLACK LITERATURE IN REVIEW: Crack, In the Downtown of a Town in Idaho and All I Wanted Was a Loaf of Bread, Bee Hive
PHATI'TUDE: In a Place Where, My People
RHAPSODY IN BLACK: Take a Lesson, Hallow Reed, Rock Me, Love's Broom
THE TEMPLE: Natural, Water aand Earth
MOUNT VOICES: SPRING THAW

ISBN 0–9661290-1-6 (Paper)

Library of Congress Catalog Card Number: 99- 94552

I dedicate this book

to the memory of my cousin

G.P. (Garnett Paul) Johnson

1957 –1997

CONTENTS

X

A NEW SENSE OF FREEDOM

African American poetry has, during the past decade, shifted toward a new framework of expression, and at the same time, has extended the tradition. What does this mean? How can this be true? There is no doubt that hip-hop has been incorporated into African American poetry, but the oral tradition is also very much alive. The basis for this argument is that emerging African American poets have a new sense of freedom to explore their own culture more in-depth and to report truth as they know it, particularly about their own communities. Such poetry speaks to the entire human race. And this assertion has contributed to increased sales of poetry books.

Patricia A. Johnson is essentially a poet who uses the freedom to explore her own culture. Her prominent subjects are family, race relations, love, and celebration of the self and African American culture. From " Somebody's Child", one of the most powerful poems in this collection:

>It's a sign of the times
>They're burning black churches in the south.
>They're burning black churches in the south.

These lines illustrate the urgency of the message. The repetition reinforces the fact that the church burnings are consistently igniting the southern nights. There is also a sense of weeping that surfaces. Johnson offers a startling assumption as to the cause of these black church burnings:

Somebody's child couldn't stand to hear
A sister hum her woes:
"Precious Lord, take my hand"

Somebody's child couldn't stand to hear
A brother pour out his soul:
"We come Father on bended knee
Humbly asking for your blessings . . . ."

Clearly these lines articulate the disturbing assumption that the persons are committing the church burnings because they can't understand that the churches were built for the praising, singing, and shouting that turn the airwaves into music. Then, too, perhaps the persons know what churches are for, but they might not care at all. Johnson lets the reader draw his or her own conclusion. And that is the way a good poem works.

Finally, in Patricia A. Johnson's **STAIN MY DAYS BLUE**, the reader can feel the passion. Yet there is much pain in her poetry, too. She reveals the truth. Line after line turns into word-songs. Listen to her work waver notes for everybody's ears.

LENARD D. MOORE
North Carolina State University

In a muddy ditch
blueberries hang so heavy
the bush falls shining.

WORD BONE

I had a word
and the word was dance
I said I had a word
and the word was dance
scratching and pecking
at the walls of my heart

I had a bone
and the bone was breath
knit one purl two
knit one purl two
weaving a web for my love
to fall into

I had a work
and the work was Word
banging and hammering
my arms into wings
and I flew, Ha-Ha!
I flew.

GABRIEL

(on meeting Lenard D. Moore)

sound that trumpet Gabriel
round, melodious, hooked
and waverly glass sound
Gabriel, sound
pink similes, blue metaphors,
green symbolism, purple meter
sound Gabriel, sound

your words
wood and stone, sand and earth
 water and air, salt and fire
sound against my flesh
resonate within my spirit
plummet down my inner cliffs
reshaping, renaming, they fall

like free cast seeds
seeking sure ground
my soul soil
turned and tilled
enfolds and tucks them
covers and wraps them
writes them down

sound Gabriel, sound
through veins that stretch
from you, to ears that hear,
hands that write
sound that trumpet Gabriel
cast your seeds
to fertile ground

SISTER MOON

she rose
before first light
slipped into the garden
in her night-shirt

bloomerless
she bent in the coolness
to pick green beans
by the last light
of a full moon

she did not want
the sun to see her
to lay his finger
rays on her shoulders
like the kisses
of an unwanted lover

sister moon
would help her
cheat him
he would not leave
his dark mark
on her honey skin

CORNMEAL MUSH

Five thirty, Monday morning
My father is in the kitchen
Making breakfast
I hear the clang of pots
The scrape and thud of wood
He puts in the stove

The smell of chicory
Climbs the steps.
I'm tempted from my cave
Beneath the quilts.
I wrap myself in broken dishes
And trip down the stairs.

Daddy stands by the stove,
Steam dances from the pan.
He pours meal
Into boiling water
Stirring, all the while,
He says, "You want some mush girl?"

SNOW CREAM

if you had told me
the winter it snowed three feet
the same day my older brother turned ten
and mama sent me out with a bowl
i filled to the brim.
she made snow cream
slick as egg white,
specially for my brother
and we sang . . .

if you had told me then
i would not have believed,
we were poor.

SOMEBODY'S CHILD

It's a sign of the times,
They're burning Black churches in the South.
They're burning Black churches in the South.

Thin haired deacons shake their heads
On bended knee at the prayer bench
Grey-haired sisters press their fists
To grim lips and hum

The old Negroes pray
Forgotten prayers
Of freedom, faith, fortitude
They wear out their knees
Refuse to wag their tongues
Or shake their fists

Somebody's child couldn't stand
To hear a sister hum her woes
" Precious Lord, take my hand"

Somebody's child couldn't stand
To hear a brother pour out his soul:
"We come Father on bended knee
 Humbly asking for your blessings.
 We ask that you bless the weak, the weary!
 We ask that you lift them up!
 Lift them up Father!"

Somebody's child couldn't stand
To hear the congregation sing praises:
"Glory! Hallelujah!
Thank you, Jesus!
Thank you, Lord"

They are burning Black churches in the South.

Looking through the smoke,
I wonder whether you see
How of a time, the walls folded up
To become the cloak that hid the run-away,
Shield that protected the unjustly accused,
Sword that defended the helpless

Sifting through the ashes,
I wonder whether you see
How of a time, church pews
Became Monday morning school desks
Preachers, political activists

Standing amidst the rubble,
I wonder whether you see
Reflected in shards of shattered glass
The generations of families
Dressed in their best
The homecomings and suppers
Served on the ground

Staring at the charred church bell,
I wonder whether you hear
The young people lift their voices
In a gospel song:
" We've come this far, by faith"
Can you see, how of a time
Choir robes replaced gang colors

Somebody' s child is being prayed for
By the membership of a church
He burned to the ground.
They pray: " Mercy, mercy!" and
" Loose, Father!
Loose from the hands of Satan"

Somebody's child
Somebody's child could have skin
Blackened by genes old as sound
Somebody's child could have started
A race war

The old Negroes sigh,
" It's a sign of the times"
They recognize,
Somebody's child
Is burning Black churches in the South.

ADDRESS UNKNOWN

Up from blue whiteness,
black wings fly against chalk sky
A dozen crows caw.
Dipping ink wings in milk clouds,
they write sealed letters to God.

PLAITS

I take matters into hand
To change my hair
Part it in rows
Clean as an Iowa cornfield
Plait it in mini-wheat squares
Fasten each end
With a bright colored barrette
Place the orange planes and
Hot pink hearts in strategic zones
Paint my lips red
Slide purple pinwheels
In my ears
Welcome the day

Strangers stop to greet me
And though I do not speak
Ukrainian, Chinese or French
I understand they are saying,
"Your hair! Your hair!"

IN THE DOWNTOWN OF A TOWN IN IDAHO AND ALL I WANTED WAS A LOAF OF BREAD

                    " Hello, sister!"
A tiny, white raccoon-eyed woman
Beamed from across the store.
                    " Welcome!" she said,
Scampering toward me
                    "It's sad they don't call you
                    Nigra or nigress anymore."
She sat her favored
Two liter bottle of liquor
On the counter, said
                    "Nigger-ress is a compliment
                    And you're tan not black"
I tried to ignore her,
                    "I love your hair."
 But she reached out,
Flipped my braids and walked away.

The cashier mumbled an apology
As he counted change into my hand.
I smile looking down
At a dollar bill with a bullet-hole in it.
I reached for my groceries and she was back
                    " Put toothpaste in the cracks nigress,
                              That's good luck."
                    " Thank you," I said to the cashier
And walked out the door
                    "So long, sister!" she yelled

I stepped into the sun
Out of a deep dark hole in Idaho
I thought, how things have changed.
I did not care to strike her,
Teach her, forgive her.
I was not bothered
By the exchange,
I did not care.

From somewhere far off
Far back as sixty-three
They welled up behind my face
Fell off the lid of my eye
And down my cheek.

NIGHT OF TWENTY-ONE WHITE TAIL

Sun vacates the sky,
without a hint of color
on the grey drape of evening.
A sixteen point buck, pauses
in the middle of the road,
looks at me . . . turns back,
joins two does on the steep bank.
Their fur blends with the colors
of bark and expanse of dead leaves.
I shudder, they leap up the hillside.
To my left, in the front yard
of the old Wingate place, three stags.
Over by the barn, burgundy
in the dusk, five does saunter.
On the hill, beside the house, three bucks,
half their racks have fallen away.
Eleven white-tail, lift their noses,
sniff the air and continue to graze.
Around the bend, seven more,
oblivious, heads down, chewing.
What is nature serving up this evening?
Who else has been invited?
I check my mirrors, there is no one
but me and twenty-one white-tail deer.

IN A PLACE WHERE

crepe myrtle hangs
brushes the ground
japanese beetles
ride each other's back
the leaf eaten
away beneath them
hills and mountains
carve out the sky
random pieces
in a rag quilt
queen anne's lace, ragweed
sweet peas and joe-pye weed
choke the roadside
there are no signs stating:

wild flowers, do not pick

in a place where
crows big as cats feed
in fields dotted
with wagon-wheel hay bales
cattle, flies sipping
from their eyes
seek shade from trees
along the fence line
in a place where
you drink a breath and
hay, manure, magnolia
clover and wild primroses

ride the intake of air
a dirt road is swallowed by pines
smoke rises above silver maples
the smell of hog killing
hangs in the air
heavy shoes crunch gravel
down and up an incline
to the trailer
offset by trash
circled by weeds

on a mattress
in front yard
crumpled and headless
a Black man burns
July 25, 1997; G.P. Johnson
was burned alive and decapitated
in rural Grayson county Virginia
in a place where
I call home.

BLACK PATENT LEATHER

I can not look up
my face reflects in your shoes
tears fall on me there
run in salt trails to the sole
form a puddle by his grave

BREATH ON MY FINGERS

There used to be a barn here
Weathered, grey and leaning.

When we were youngins,
Waiting for the school bus
In bone-cold weather

We'd slip behind a loose board
Into the breath-warmed barn,
Stand ankle-deep in straw

Half-fearing the cows
That were our redemption.

HALLOW REED

i am Hallow Reed
you are Fierce Wind
have mercy
flow through me
and i will sing
unashamed!
have mercy
make of me
an instrument
of joy
together
in music
we are
poetry.

SISTERS

Church ladies
knees part
from years
of holding a man

Glory!

she sits on
the front row
white and grey
head bobbing

I ask, "how
did you get
so strong?"
she says,
"Well, there was
Mama
and I did
such stupid things
I let people
use me."

Church ladies
lips part
to praise
God

Hallelujah!

she sits close
to the door
stretched belly
skirts her knees

I ask"how
did you get
so wise?"
she says
"I listened
to Mama
and I wasn't
real smart
I let people
hurt me."

Church ladies
lift their arms
sagging flesh
trembles

Thank you Lord!

she sits near
the open window
blind eyes shaded
wig askew

I ask,"how
did you get
so patient and kind?"

she says,"Whatever
Mama said, I did
the opposite
I knew it all
and then too
I allowed people
to abuse me."

Church ladies
soulful voices
ride air
between here
and eternity

Glory!

I remember
their Mama
straight and
wizened, wise
and strong.

WITNESS

Wind blows light in flames
down the valley bottom,
licks its frigid tongue
against the mountain and laughs.
I am awake to witness.

shafts of amber, light
maggots, on a smokehouse ham
white roses wilt

ECLIPSE

I watch the night
chew up a full glowing moon
I say nothing.
Just stand, perfectly still,
trying not to bat my eyes.

CHAIRMAN OF THE BAR

(black and white photo, circa 1940 *)*

Caged light bulbs
illumine the bar
polished, shiny as a chestnut
just released from its burr.
The doors open in ten minutes;
beer, liquor and wine are stocked
with triple back-ups, high out of reach.
Pickles, pig feet and pickled eggs,
potato chips and pig skins a plenty.
Rubbed beer mugs gleam like prisms.
Dr. Poindexter, in pressed whites,
has inspected his staff.
Three brown skin sisters in white
uniforms, one redbone in burgundy.
Their bodices are pinned,
there will be no overflowing
cleavage on his shift.

Lips pressed thin, he is in charge.
Jim Crow does not respect
the PhD. hanging on his wall
but when these doors open
Dr. Poindexter is,
Chairman of the bar.

CRYSTAL

Aunt Minnie's sepia photo
Slips from shames' hiding place
Beneath the dresser drawer
My eyes meet hers

White muslin blouse
Pierced by thorns
Stained by her blood
Lays open

Aunt Minnie
Black Madonna
A white rose cups
Her milk engorged breast
From her coal black nipple
A string of liquid pearls
Meets the open mouth

Aunt Minnie's Face
Slick with sweat
Eyes, dry lake beds
The fruit of her loins
Auctioned, like cattle
To fill Massa's
China cabinet
With glass.

THERE WAS NO MIXING OF THE RACES

She had a truth I wanted to know,
My history was lost
The names of my people
Hushed on the lips of the dead.
She had a truth I wanted to know
The truth was in front of her,
How did I come to be?

There was no mixing of the races

She wanted to believe
He was a kind man, a good man,
A honorable man.
Time nulls the whispers,
How her great-great-great Pa dressed
My great-great Ma in fancy clothes
Seeded her a son, then sold her away
When he was only three.
They dragged her off,
Him screaming and crying,
Holding on to her skirt so strong
They had to cut him away.

There was no mixing of the races

Great Aunt E, a girl of twelve or so
Was sent to help an ailing wife,
Cook, clean, care for the children
The husband took her to warm his bed,

A diaper in her mouth
No one heard her screams.
When his deed could be seen.
She was sent back to her kin.

There was no mixing of the races

She had a truth I wanted to know,
Who begot who and when.
He was a good man, a kind man,
An honorable man.
She placed a Bible in my hands:
>   *Record of Blacks*
>   *Age of the Collard*
>   *Record of the Coulerd Family of*
>   *Record of the Children of the Coulard*
My peoples' names exchanged for a lie

There was no mixing of the races.

MY PEOPLE

Earth passes over my fingers
And I feel my ancestors
Pass through them

My feet sink into the land
I cannot tell where we end
Earth the color of my skin
God made me of yellow clay
From this West lot of Eden
Carrier of the water bowl
I turn my face within

Cousin Letcher with blue gums
Comes from that patch
A few feet South
Soil rich and dark as oil
He sounds with the wind
The rhythms of our soul
Keeper of the drum

Uncle with no name
White, bloodless
Rises up in the North
Like a dead man from the sand
Where creeping vines crawl
Roots bleached in the sun
He holds the mirror

Grandma Bones
Weaving spider panes
Comes from that bank
Sporting red clay in slates
Carrier of fire
Rising in the East
She sings to our spirit

Blood of this land
Water of these creeks
Dust and ground bone

My people.

LOVE'S BROOM

Walls come a tumbling,
Walls come a tumbling, down.
In the face of love,
Walls come a crumbling,
Walls come a crumbling, down
Before the face of love
A soul cries out
And walls crack, walls crack!
Love makes room
Where there is no room,
Doorways where there are no ways,
Love will have its way.

Run run, but you can't hide
From love's tracking eyes
Flee, flee, where you gonna be,
Where is it that love can't find you?
Work, work, build a stronger wall
Love will sweep it aside.
Sweep it aside.
Under the shadow of love's broom
Walls fall,
They all fall down.
Love reigns,
Love reigns supreme.

SWEET FREEDOM

I go out and knock
snow from her tender brown limbs,
hear her freedom cry
as she springs up from the ground
soaking me in crystal tears.

CALLING FOR SNOW

The green of mustard
And turnip shine above
A throw-rug of snow
Brighter and darker
Than dull, light
Summer greens.

The ground soft,
Swollen and spilling
Clings to my boots
Then sighs away.
I bend over the patch
Break a curly leaf
The smell swallows me

I am transported
to Mammaw's kitchen
apron skirting
a ladder-back
blue enamel dipper
hanging on a galvanized pail
a kettle of greens
boiling on the stove
laughter seeping
from the lid
hot water cornbread
frying with ham hock
mince-meat pie cooling
on the safe

I inhale
My way back to the garden
Brown earth, green mustard
And turnip leaves shining
Bend and break
Bend and break

THE KINK FELL OUT OF MY HAIR

They killed G.P. and the kink fell out of my hair
He was my cousin, blood brother, bond of felicity.
They said, "Another nigger dead; white folks don't care."

Here a Negro not knowing his place is rare,
Been trained since slavery to smile, nod, and agree.
They killed G.P. and the kink fell out of my hair

Four white people and broken black G.P. unaware
That party was his garden of Gethsemane.
They said, "Another nigger dead; white folks don't care."

Trussed like a pig, doused in gasoline, set afire.
White cross or clothesline T, it was a gallows tree.
They killed G.P. and the kink fell out of my hair

Reeling in the blaze, only his body for pyre,
A maul extinguished his plea, "Why don't you shoot me?!"
They said, " Another nigger dead; white folks don't care."

Like rain in the desert, dissipates, so did his air
They hewed him, hacked his head off, then watched TV
They killed G. P. and the kink fell out of my hair
They said, "Another nigger dead; white folks don't care."

FIFTY THOUSAND DOLLARS

Behind the bar on the first row,
 his parents face the judge's bench.
Vertebrae pressed into maple,
 you can tell they don't go out much,
 work their jobs then go home and labor.
The father wears coveralls and flannel,
 silver beard ripples across his chest,
 blue eyes travel heavenward in their caverns.
The mother, a cowlick, wearing
 polyester imprinted with her bones.
Her face, a drying apple, embedded eyes
search the floor corner to corner.
They've come about taking their boy home,
offering all they have as his bond.
He is their son; they want him back,
no matter that another man's son
 has been bagged, boxed and buried.

BITTER WHITE APPLES

the crab, apple tree's naked branches
scratch sky-blue, blue sky
she holds fast to her fruit
high and deep within their thorny boughs
I trade blood and scars
for tiny, bitter, white apples

cook them whole
strain juice, add sugar
boil rolling, pour hot
pink liquid into sterilized
glass jelly jars, cool
seal with wax to keep.

I write on each label
acquired at high cost, use sparingly

CITY ON THE VINE

soon as the waters recede
I go looking
for the city on the vine
I came across it
in my walks
watched its citizens
enter and exit
through its single gate

between raspberry and pine
hanging in mid-air
grey as worn asphalt
a city built for a queen
around a thorny vine
anchored by a fence post
the rose bush climbs.

I walk the grass braid
swaying the dirt road's middle
troughs of mud on either side
my eyes scan the fence
find the vine still there
clinging.
my feet sink into
pine-blackened hillside

among needles and leaves
the city lies in pewter layers
empty.
mud dries in cakes on my legs
as I watch paper wasps
rebuild their city
on the vine.

TAKE A LESSON

stand on the beach
in one place
soon
the water comes
and the sand goes
the water comes
and the sand goes
you go deeper
and deeper

still
the water comes
the sand goes
till the water
is all around you
only your head is free
and the water comes
the sand goes till the water
is all over you
holding your breath
and the water comes
the sand goes

still
you stand
in one place
you are going
to drown
take a lesson
from the sand
water comes
go with it.

JUSTICE NAPS AT A SLOT MACHINE IN VEGAS

Justice reached down its big oak hand
scaled with lichen
and squeezed
cries from a black mama,
high, high
as a crickets' call;
cries from grand-daddy,
low, low
as a bullfrogs' croak.
Reached down fingers
like a noose
knotted rope round her
tawny, tendril throat
and squeezed
till her tongue popped out.

Jesus,
the pain singes
like fire
licking wet skin,
like a woman
at the rear of a church
got Jesus blowing on her back,
like Oklahoma City

standing by a fence
littered with grief
like Elk Creek, Virginia
and Jasper, Texas
burying headless black men,
and justice naps
at a slot machine in Vegas

MANNA

Branch cress has fallen, weighted down with
      seeds
Strawberries drop, drained of their wild
      sweetness
Rhubarb's tall, tart stalks dry to hollow reeds
Creecy greens' flower explodes lemon zest
Cheery branches drag the ground, fruit laden
Plantain and rat tail toughen in the field
Poke salad leaves shade red berries' toxin
Snakes sleep in the berry patch on the hill
I remember picking the first spring greens
Collecting raspberries in syrup cans
Mama boiling roots, bark and herbs for cures
Carefully using the gifts of the land.
Now Boneset, a cold remedy, grows
      unfound
Burdock's healing root remains in the
      ground.

CONJURER WOMAN

I was a muddy brown girl nearing five years old
Seething like a pot left too long on the stove
I was thin as a cornstalk but not near as tall
The other children called me names
Bullied me, chased and cornered me
The terror rose in my mouth like bile
I snatched hair from each of their heads
Dug ragged fingernails into flesh
And drug away bits of their skin
Bruised and sore, I ran to Daddy's tater patch
Laid down between the rows
Their leaves a dark canopy shielding me

O hush be still hush be still

The tears came, jerking my body
Like a sapling in the wind
The earth catching me, holding me
Whispered hushed instructions into my hair
I rose with a tater in my hand
That I carved and filled with the hair,
Skin and blood from under nails
Chanting all the while
The ends of my hair crisp
I burrowed a hole, dropped the tater in
Blew the dirt to cover

O hush be still hush be still

The moon dropped past the mountain
The sun rose streaking the sky
Sweet bell pepper red
Behind a flock of mamas and papas, cousins and
        aunts
Who couldn't rouse bullying children from their
        beds
A doctor unable to explain their crusted eyes
Theft of breath and stumbling steps
Nothing left they could do but send for HER
Her, the one they needed and feared
Warned us children to steer clear of
The lady of hips and scarves
Scents and weeds, they sent for her
To point to the conjurer

O hush be still hush be still

She come
In long gathered skirt, crocheted shawl
Head wrapped and tied in printed folds
Stood in the clearing looking on the flock
She parted us like pressed hair
Walked around me three times
Circling me with lavender, honey, tarragon
Looked through me to the tater patch
I saw her see me there and all I done
She flew to my keeping place
And with one breath
Exposed it

O hush be still hush be still

She lifted her finger and pointed at me
I was the one
And it had to be beaten out
"I was doing what my hair said,
Just the way ground told it!" I said
But there was cotton in the ears
Boulders on the path
A cloud across the sun
The birches bled for me
Wild azaleas wept
Dogwoods screamed

O hush

BONE RATTLE

I am.
I am not alone,
Kenetta, Alice and Allyne
Walk with me.

I am.
I am not alone,
Sally Alverna, Lanny and Lucy
Walk with me.

I am.
I am not alone,
Nancy Caroline, Eula and Eva
Walk with me.

I am.
I am not alone,
The voices of my elders
Talk with me, guide and comfort me.
The bones of Conley, Daley and Reece
Rattle in my voice
Bones that have been turned
In the sun and fired
Still they ring, sound
Against ear-drum, heart-drum
Is drum . . .

I am.
I am not alone,
The angels of my foreparents
Keep me from harm.
Edmond, Calvin and James
Come bearing bowls
Filled with ground bone
They blow in words
Over my spirit.

I am.
I am not alone,
See me and you see we,
Centha, Mary and Millie
Walk with me.

QUAKING ASH

sometimes I have to fold
myself up and hold on tight
till the quake runs through

you may not touch me then

parts of my self
may fall at your feet
like leaves, coin-shaped
gold

cells of myself
may be carried away
on your hands like
ash

there are times
only God can hold me
in the sound
stream

my mouth waters
poison oak lines the steep bank
full of black berries

I REMEMBER A TIME
I THOUGHT I WAS BETTER THAN THEM

They wrapped their legs
In rainbow rags torn into strips
Covered their walls in newspaper print
Collected the organs at hog killing time
Inviting everyone for dinner,
Lights and chittlins,
Breakfast of brains and eggs.

Their bag lunches had grease spots;
The deer meat, rabbit or squirrel
Dropped in without wax-paper wrapping
In leaner times without bread.

I always spoke, never stared . . .

Twenty years later,
I open a package from thenm
A complimentary copy of their award winning
Bestseller, **Road-kill or Delicacy**
Signed with this note:

You were always so nice.

NATURAL

Girlfriend, Girlfriend
I walked into the nineties
With my sixties' natural
Still bobbing in the wind.

After twenty years
People recognized me
Through fifty pounds
And swore I had not changed.
I went from size 12 to size 18
But I had not changed.

I traded in my militancy for two degrees
My bell-bottom jeans for a pin-striped suit
Mind expanding drugs for Zen meditation
Exchanged my virginity for celibacy
But I had not changed
Because my hairstyle remained the same.

I refused to alter it even though security
Followed me around department stores.
Police officers did U-turns on busy streets,
Drew their weapons before approaching my vehicle.
After calling for back-up, they would detain me,
Try to match me with a crime.
Aggravated when I was not a radical
just one crazy female who couldn't keep up
With the fashion times.

In '93 I succumbed to the chemicals
Screaming and crying like a boy in a barber's chair
I emerged with shoulder-length dark-brown hair
that got on my nerves even though
I had that white girl flip going on.
I had to cut it off,
It felt like something was crawling on me.

And then I discovered my scalp
The hair, finger-snapping short
Rub it across the grain,
Felt like ten men breathing on my neck,
A G-spot I could touch in public

But I missed my fro, my natural, my bush.
I dyed it blonde and let it grow. Honey!
Men followed these 42 inch hips down the street
Phone numbers in hand begging,
That yellow hair had to go.

Six months in braids
I'm back where I started
Just as nappy and kinky as I wanna be
Strutting my natural
And it's back in style again.

GOOD SEED

The first snow has fallen,
ice clings to tree limbs,
hangs in icicles from roofs.
The mailman backs up our dead-end dirt road
stops at each box on his way down.
I cross the half-acre of yard
leaving dips in the unbaked meringue
Bootsie at my heels, her black fur
shines like patent leather.

A mass of color spills from the box,
seed catalogues
arrive daily since the first frost,
two and three at a time, some in duplicate
Burpee and Gurney's have free gifts,
Shumways: "good seed cheap";
Vermont Bean: "seeds from the world"
Territorial Seed requests that we:
"Plant a row for the hungry."

George Johnson reads each one,
flipping pages back to his Daddy's home place.
A syrup can dangles from his palm. He picks
blackberries, raspberries, strawberries,
blueberries, until he turns the page.
He feels the weight of the zucchini,
heat of sun in the tomatoes and laughs out loud.
Carefully, he chooses seed, places orders,
plots a garden better than the last.

SPRING THAW

Listening to the sound
of the creek
lap-dancing with rocks
and the hum of the tractor
on the hill
makes the burn
in my calves worthwhile.
A butterfly summer-saults
as it skirts too close
and the breeze kisses
sweat on my face.

I look past the yellow
flowering heads of creecy greens
past the fields of alfalfa
soon to be cut
past the green thimble hills
to the blue mountains
I wonder about
refractions of light
that take green, brown, gray
and turn them
to purplish blue.

Reaching the knoll of the hill
I rub my calves and thighs
bend in the middle
rest my hands on my knees.
The hiss of my breath

rhythmic clap of my heart
plop of my sweat
into the dust
of the gravel road
are the sounds
of my creek.

THIRD SUNDAY IN JUNE

Black-heart cherries ready,
third Sunday in June,
you can depend on it.
In the upper branches
of Mr. Clay's tree,
two Sundays early,
I am pulling cherries
off in clumps.
Black heart's juice
runs sticky, warm
trails down my arm.
My tongue catches
sun-warmed sweetness.

I am here before the worms
and birds take their fill,
careful to leave the unripe
just as Butch left me,
hanging, green and blushing.
He will be back
third Sunday in June
you can depend on it . . .

I gather enough black hearts
to make a pie for supper
with some left over
for cherries' jubilee
when the first snow falls.

STAIN MY DAYS BLUE

What's a woman to do
Once she's loved a man like you

With the color of you everywhere
Staining my days blue

Tell me
What's a woman to do

I taste you in the water
Cupped to my lips

Smell you in the steam
From the oatmeal on the stove

Hear you in the breeze
Through the Joe-pye weed

Tell me
What's a woman to do

You brought me to my knees
Stuttering and cooing like a dove

Your arms tattooed around
From my shoulders to my ankles

Your lips left third degree burns
On the back of my neck

Down to the balls of my feet
Your breath the only healing balm

Oh, tell me
What's a woman to do

Once she's loved a man
Like you

NEVER THE SAME PLACE TWICE

I am rooted
of the earth
You are free
lightning bolt
come down
splitting me asunder
spiraling a scream
setting off fires
sating them with rain
whipping the wind
sowing seed
in a garden
I will tend

SPOON

my bed is just a bed
without you here

to press into my back
to weave your fingers
through the ropes of my hair
to brush your lips
a breeze across my neck
to lay me in the spoon
   of your body
and rock me into sleep
to the rhythm of your
   heartbeat . . .

without you here
it's just a bed

CRACK

Flying into love
A loose rock hits my windshield,
Breaks up my heart.

BEE-HIVE

I remember the pain,
Crumpled like tin foil
Around leftovers.
I remember hurting
Balled up on the floor
Rattling like spooked chimes
My eyes, lakes, spilling
Over swollen banks.

He traded
Soft arms that held him
For wire mesh filter,
Warm thighs that cradled him
For steel piping

He left salt
Trails on my face,
Craters in my heart,
For the distant embrace
Of a crack pipes'
Frigid phantoms.

I remember the pain
Fresh
As taking honey from a hive
Still,
I want him.

NOTHING SNAPPED

I have thought about it,
it's not how people say:
"Her mind snapped,"
There was no snapping.

Light sliced through my mind
like blue flame through tin.

It was cool and quick
as a school of minnow
chased by trout.

I was altered
like twisted sheets
pulled crisp as saltines,
a knotted chain melted
straight as hard-pressed hair
till tired Wednesday

ain't nothing but change
in Sundays' offering plate.

I looked at white against brown
my arms circled in soap suds;
brown against white,
butcher knife on enamel sink.

What's the worst that could happen?
They could execute me,
I can handle that.

Knife in hand, I grew bigger
than love. Body met the walls,
head brushed ceiling, every pore
seeping. My nostrils, vacuums
inhaling fear, bits of spirit,
flakes of skin, strands of hair

I intended to spill his blood

SPIRIT HUES

You dip your fingers
Into my soul, spread
Spirit colors cross the sky.
Purple, crimson and gold
Swirl in ribbon shawls,
Dance like lone sisters
Meeting again. Arms cross
Legs criss, skirts fling,
Square dancers stirring sawdust
Jumping, turning, in one dash
Landing with toe pointed up.
My soul arches into a smile
Pulse grows staccato
You are gone.
Scissors cut against sky
Liquid spirit hues bleed tissue
Drop like confetti at my feet
No matter how often I sweep
In a week I find another piece.

WATER AND EARTH

I wanted my husband
Smelling like a black man.
So, I changed his diet,
Fed him cornbread, greens and yams,
Slipped in palm oil and cayenne, when I could.
Washed his clothes in Oxydol,
Bathed him in Ivory soap,
Rubbed him in coco and shea butters,
Shampooed his hair in coconut,
Laid it back with Royal Crown,
That man was smelling so good,
I called him Negro.
Three days I wallowed
In his aromatic trough

Before his body revolted,
Purged itself . . .
Cayenne blazed a trail
Through his lower tract,
Whelps snaked on his scalp,
Red splotches mushroomed on his skin,
Pimples and blackheads rioted on his face,
I had to stop
I had married water
There was no way
To lay earth on it.

ROCK ME

I am going to take hold of myself
    and rock me
Rock me to the depths of myself
Push me up out of myself

Spread a rainbow of myself over you
Hear you catch your breath . . . and
Rock me back into myself
    and sigh . . .

RESPONSE TO A COMPLIMENT FROM A WHITE FRIEND

"You're not really black,
You talk and act like a white person,
listening to country music,
I've seen your cowboy boots.
You're not like 'them,' you're the whitest
black person I know."

If I am not black,
what was that little girl
who attended Independence Colored School?
A two room school with a pair of teachers,
twin pot stoves and a couple outdoor toilets.

If I am not black,
What was that adolescent
who integrated Grayson County High School?
what was that teenage girl
who was the first Negro
cheerleader in Independence, Virginia.

If I am not black,
what was that young woman,
who sang, "We shall over come"
louder than anybody and off key?
Shouted, "I'm black and I'm proud!"
and " Kill whitey! Kill whitey!"

If I am not black,
why was I the last patient seen
with burns so severe, the skin hung from my face?
" First come, first served, emergencies first"
were reserved for another race.

If I am not black,
why was that job available,
the apartment vacant
when we conversed on the phone
but when I arrived, they were gone?

If I am not black,
what was that woman
cooking up neckbones and collard greens,
sweet potatoe pie and black-eyed peas.
singing and crying listening to BB King?

If I am not black,
what was that woman wrestling
her kinky hair into braids
trying to tame a jungle?

Lucky for you, I know Jesus
You couldn't handle me
getting Black on you

SPIRIT RISING

naked, i
move
through transformation
wake liquid fields
before the veiled forest
that harbors
my dreams, i
choose one, place
it in the pocket of my spirit
i am buoyed , lifted.
from behind skirted boughs, i
hear secret laughter beating
like a bird trapped against glass
falling . . . i
wrap myself in dry leaves
the wind kisses them and strips me, i
sway forward, back, cannot
       go
till the whispers hush,and i
hush the shush of them
against fatted thighs and puffed cheeks
against licked lips and beaded palms
against starched neck and leather ear, i
shusha shusha hush them
like a hoofer tapping in sawdust
step, ball/change; step, ball/change
ball/change, ball/change, i
tap out the gnawing
red ant doubts, the crippling

termite fears
that crawl, bore beneath bark,
the fiber of my dream
summoning the beetles
my spirit invokes them,
they lend me their wings
and from the dung, i
ascend

IN MY FATHER'S HOUSE

If I could, I'd tell you how light fills my room
in the morning, teasing me out of bed. I would tell you about
standing at the kitchen window watching the sun crest treetops,
casting an amber glow on the dawn. Somedays,
screaming streaks of red with shocks of pink
cause my jaw to drop, breath to stop. Other mornings,
orange lays atop black clouds shouldered by saffron rays
so majestically, I run out and bow down the earth.

I'd tell you about walking the sun-warmed garden
bare-foot after it's been turned by the plough.
Pushing my feet down till earth engulfs my ankles
squiggle my toes through the top like budding plants
whiff the soil's deep, dark, hearty musk.
Lay off rows, watch the moon, sow seed,
bless each one to grow strong and fruitful.

I would tell you about lying in grass
hanging my head and arms over the bank
to cup the coldest sweetest water
ever pushed to surface by a spring.
I'd tell you about my grandma collecting yellow tommy-toes
yelling over her shoulder "get up from there, you'll get chiggers."

I'd tell you about honeysuckle riding red Virginia banks,
pulling a pistil through its blossom
for a drop of nectar no bigger than a tear. On the tongue
it's golden-honey, crystal-water and sun.
I'd tell you about apple, pear and cherry tree blooming.

Take a blossom from each and I cannot tell one from the other,
only that they are fruits not nuts. I would tell you about my parents
81 and 79 leaning against each other to stand without canes.

Sitting under the tree I picked it from, I bite into an apple;
its juice splashes my face. I would tell you about
walking into the hills with a bucket I hope to fill
with wild raspberries, blackberries or blueberries.
The berry's flavor sharpened by its pungent aroma
and slick feel in my mouth. Jesus, if I only had words enough,
tears enough, laugher enough, I would tell you
about the magnificence of God.

SHATTERED

She is broken
Riddled as honeycomb
I found a piece of her
Under the bed
In her husband's Sunday shoes.
He never wears them,

Not even when her Mama died.

Three more pieces
In the sifter
Tight against the screen,
I could have baked her,
Sopped up the gravy
With a piece of her in the roll.

Rolls have no taste since her sister Dot passed.

In the dog's basket
of chew toys,
A jagged piece . . .
Thin as egg shell
Caught in the lattice weave.

On a white cross charred crisp, her godson's body

She is broken
Shattered, scattered
To the four directions,
Moths polish the last tooth.

Disease rocks her, wins at hide and seek

I find another piece
Add it to the collection.
Like a blind man
I fit them together
Under a new moon.

RON-RON

Heat laid across the days and nights
Of a Maine September like a quilt
On an iron bed in an Appalachian mountain cabin.
A moist heat that refused to let clothes dry
On the line or sweat to evaporate from skin.
His body's dew soaked the crispness
From another linen shirt

The energy used to change it
Exhausting his limbs, reminding me
He was dying
My eyes looked into his but would not see
AIDS ravaged pools
He looked the same to me, sounded and felt
The same.

He was cut crystal, intricate and refined
I was blown glass
Simple as a breath exhaled
Simple, as his final exit.

COME AND SEE

(A poem for Dorian and Swede on their wedding day)

Drought in my heart, sand in my mouth
Denying the wind and all unseen
This is what is.
What is it that I do not know?
You said to me

Come and see

I was afraid but could not resist
Your pull on the fibers fringing my heart
My eyes followed bringing body beside
Honeycomb and apple blossom bed
You looked through my turquoise web
Stirred the ashes of spirit in me
Blew across temple tablets tripping fire
Scales slipped away like molt, rose in smoke

Come and see

In my heart stand six stone waterpots
Like oak trunks, hollow and empty
Our children fill one then another
Till all, run over the lip lapping water
Music flows through the waterpots,
Rises through pain, erodes fear
Your spirit touches my inside
Infuses my being with light

Come and see

Water turned to wine, the best, poured last
So is this love turned from water
Poured after all else was well savored
The good kept until now
This love, a rod in the desert
Lifted up, separating the waters
As God loves the world
I love you

Come and see